POINTS OF VIEW

Should PEANUTS Be Banned in Schools?

By Simon Pierce

KidHaven PUBLISHING

Published in 2022 by
KidHaven Publishing, an Imprint of Greenhaven Publishing, LLC
353 3rd Avenue
Suite 255
New York, NY 10010

Designer: Deanna Paternostro
Editor: Jennifer Lombardo

Photo credits: Cover Sean Locke Photography/Shutterstock.com; p. 5 (main) gilaxia/E+/Getty Images; p. 5 (inset) Andy Sacks/The Image Bank/Getty Images; p. 7 MSPhotographic/iStock/Getty Images Plus/Getty Images; p. 9 Bloomberg/Bloomberg/Getty Images; p. 11 SolStock/E+/Getty Images; p. 13 stefanamer/iStock/Getty Images Plus/Getty Images; p. 15 (top right) KK Tan/Shutterstock.com; p. 15 (bottom left) baibaz/Shutterstock.com; p. 15 (bottom right) PixelsEffect/E+/Getty Images; p. 17 barbaragibbbons/iStock/Getty Images Plus/Getty Images; p. 19 Science Photo Library/Science Photo Library/Getty Images; p. 21 (notepad) ESB Professional/Shutterstock.com; p. 21 (markers) Kucher Serhii/Shutterstock.com; p. 21 (photo frame) FARBAI/iStock/Thinkstock; p. 21 (inset, left) AFP/Stringer/AFP/Getty Images; p. 21 (inset, left middle) John D. Buffington/DigitalVision/Getty Images Plus/Getty Images; p. 21 (inset, right middle) Boston Globe/Contributor/Boston Globe/Getty Images; p. 21 (inset, right) steele2123/iStock/Getty Images Plus/Getty Images.

Library of Congress Cataloging-in-Publication Data

Names: Pierce, Simon, author.
Title: Should peanuts be banned in schools? / Simon Pierce.
Description: New York : KidHaven Publishing, 2022. | Series: Points of view | Includes index.
Identifiers: LCCN 2020030814 | ISBN 9781534536395 (library binding) | ISBN 9781534536371 (paperback) | ISBN 9781534536388 (set) | ISBN 9781534536401 (ebook)
Subjects: LCSH: School children–Nutrition. | Peanuts. | Schools.
Classification: LCC RJ206 .P54 2022 | DDC 613.2083–dc23
LC record available at https://lccn.loc.gov/2020030814

Printed in the United States of America

Some of the images in this book illustrate individuals who are models. The depictions do not imply actual situations or events.

CPSIA compliance information: Batch #CS22KH: For further information contact Greenhaven Publishing LLC, New York, New York at 1-844-317-7404.

CONTENTS

Understanding ALLERGIES

One of the most common food allergies people have is an allergy to peanuts. When someone has an allergy, their body mistakes something harmless for something unsafe. Their body then tries to attack it, but this attack hurts the body. They have what's called an allergic reaction.

A **mild** peanut allergy might cause a stomachache or a runny nose. Someone with a **severe** allergy can have a reaction called anaphylaxis. This is when someone has trouble breathing and swallowing. If they don't get help quickly, they can die. Because of this, some people believe it's not safe to have peanuts in schools.

Know the Facts!

About 1.8 million kids in the United States have a peanut allergy.

Someone who has a peanut allergy has to read food labels very carefully. Even eating something that was made near a food that has peanuts in it could cause an allergic reaction.

Why Ban PEANUTS?

Someone with a mild peanut allergy is generally OK as long as they don't actually eat peanuts. However, someone with a severe allergy can get very sick even if they only sit close to peanuts or foods made with them. This is why some schools ban peanuts, which means they don't let kids bring anything with peanuts in it for lunch or snacks.

Some people think it's a good idea to ban peanuts because they can kill someone with a severe allergy. Other people say it's not fair to tell kids who aren't allergic what they can and can't bring for lunch.

Know the Facts!

Something a person is allergic to is called an allergen.

Peanut butter can be very messy. If someone gets it on their lunch table and doesn't clean it up, someone with an allergy who's sitting at the same table could accidentally get it on their food or clothes.

Keeping Kids SAFE

The biggest reason people support a peanut ban is because they want to keep kids safe. So many kids have peanut allergies that some people think it's smart to make it easier for these kids to avoid this food.

People who support a ban understand that most kids aren't trying to make their classmates sick on purpose. However, accidents happen. Someone might bring in a food that they don't even realize has peanuts in it. For example, some potato chips are fried in peanut oil. Many people think a ban would make students more careful about what they bring to school.

Know the Facts!

As of 2020, a two-pack of EpiPens cost between $300 and $650.

When someone has an allergic reaction, an EpiPen (shown here) can save their life. However, not everyone can afford an EpiPen, and some people don't have theirs with them at all times. This is why some people say peanut bans are the best way to keep everyone with a peanut allergy safe.

Bans Don't WORK

People who oppose peanut bans say they don't actually make kids safer. First, it's very hard to **enforce** a peanut ban. Teachers don't have time to look at all the food everyone brings for lunch every day and read all the labels to make sure there are no peanuts in any of the foods.

Second, **research** has shown that peanut bans haven't lowered the number of kids who have to go to the nurse for an allergic reaction. Making some tables in the lunchroom peanut-free has been a much more successful **policy** than banning peanuts completely.

Know the Facts!

Only 1 percent of people with a peanut allergy, or about 452,000 people, are so severely allergic that they can't smell or touch peanuts without having a reaction.

Research shows that peanut-free lunch tables are a more effective, or successful, way to keep kids safe than peanut-free schools.

Social PROBLEMS

Some people support a peanut ban because they worry about the social effects of a peanut allergy. Even with peanut-free tables, kids with a peanut allergy might end up having to eat lunch alone. This might make it harder for them to make friends.

Sometimes people don't think about the danger of an allergy, so they might joke around or bully someone by putting peanuts near them. If peanuts were banned from schools, not just from certain classrooms or lunchroom tables, kids might not feel left out, **isolated**, or bullied because of their allergy.

Know the Facts!

About one-third of kids who have a food allergy say they've been bullied. Bullying actions include making fun of someone and joking about or actually giving someone the food they're allergic to.

Some people say banning peanuts in schools could make it easier for kids with an allergy to make friends and make it less likely for them to be bullied.

Not Fair to OTHERS

Many people who oppose a peanut ban say it isn't fair to kids who don't have allergies. They say it's up to the person with the allergy to make sure they stay away from peanuts. They don't think it's right to tell other kids what they can or can't eat for lunch.

Some parents also say it's not fair to them because it makes it harder for them to pack lunch for their kids. Peanuts are very **nutritious**, and peanut butter doesn't cost much. It can be hard for a parent to find a healthy, cheap **substitute**.

Know the Facts!

Peanuts or peanut shells can be found even in some things that aren't food, such as some kinds of birdseed, makeup, and cleaning products.

There are a lot of foods that either have peanuts in them or are made near peanut products. Some people say it's not fair to kids without allergies to tell them they can't bring any of these foods to school.

Feeling BETTER

Some people say it's important for kids with a peanut allergy to feel more comfortable at school. If the school bans peanuts, they might worry less about whether they'll have an allergic reaction. Being less worried means they can pay better attention in class.

Banning peanuts also means kids with an allergy don't have to remember to ask everyone around them what's in the food they're eating. It can be hard for a kid to read everything on a food label, and they might miss a word and accidentally **expose** someone with an allergy to peanuts.

Know the Facts!

In the United States, peanut allergies are the number one cause of food-related deaths.

Anaphylaxis is very scary, both for the person having the reaction and the people around them. Banning peanuts from schools might make everyone less worried about this happening.

A Slippery SLOPE

Some people think banning peanuts is a slippery slope. This means they think it'll lead to other allergens being banned. For example, some people are allergic to milk, so maybe milk will be the next thing banned. Many people with peanut allergies also have tree nut allergies. Should tree nuts be banned too?

Some people take the slippery slope idea very far and say that soon, no food will be allowed in schools. Most people agree this won't actually happen, but the point they're trying to make is that it's hard to know where to draw the line on food bans.

Know the Facts!

Along with peanuts, the most common food allergens are cow's milk; eggs; tree nuts, such as hazelnuts and almonds; shellfish, such as crabs and shrimp; wheat; soy; and fish.

Some people argue that it doesn't make sense to ban peanuts if schools aren't going to ban the other most common food allergens.

What Do You THINK?

Everyone wants kids with allergies to be safe at school. That's why some people say keeping peanuts out of schools is important. However, others say a peanut ban isn't the best way to keep kids safe. Research shows that banning peanuts doesn't make kids less likely to have an allergic reaction at school.

Now that you know both sides of the argument, what do you think? Does having or not having a peanut allergy have an effect on your opinion? What do you think is the best way to make sure school is both safe and fair for everyone?

Know the Facts!

The number of people with peanut allergies has been **increasing** over time. In 2017, about 2.5 percent of all American kids under 18 had a peanut allergy—21 percent more than in 2010.

Should peanuts be banned in schools?

YES

- It could save someone's life.
- Kids' health is the most important thing to think about.
- Kids with a peanut allergy will be bullied less and feel less isolated.
- Kids will worry less about their allergy, which will help them pay better attention in class.

NO

- Research shows that school-wide bans don't work as well as peanut-free lunch tables.
- It's up to the person with the allergy to take care of their own health, not up to the people around them.
- It's not fair to tell allergy-free kids what they can and can't eat at school.
- Banning peanuts is a slippery slope that will lead to other food bans.

Making sure kids with peanut allergies are safe at school can be tricky. Not everyone agrees on whether or not peanut bans help.

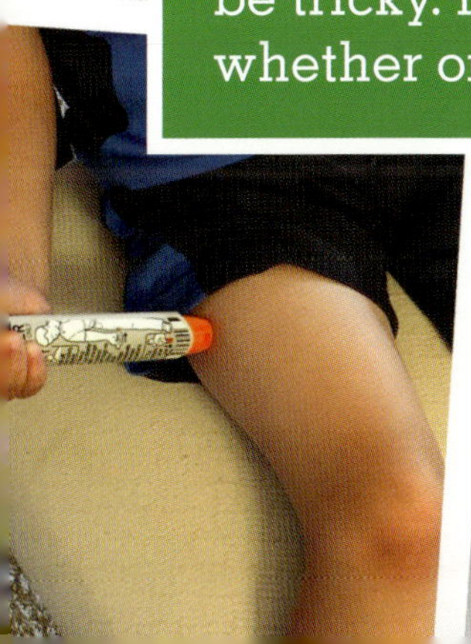

GLOSSARY

enforce: To make sure people do what is required by a rule or law.

expose: To cause someone to come into contact with something, especially something harmful.

increase: To become larger or more numerous.

isolated: Put or kept in a place that is separate from others.

mild: Not strong in action or effect.

nutritious: Having substances that a person or animal needs to be healthy and grow properly.

policy: A set of rules for how something is to be done.

research: Careful study that is done to find and report new knowledge about something.

severe: Very bad or unpleasant; causing a lot of pain or suffering.

substitute: A person or thing that takes the place of someone or something else.

For More INFORMATION

WEBSITES

Allergy Facts for Kids
kids.kiddle.co/Allergy
Explore more about allergies on this online encyclopedia entry, which includes useful facts and pictures.

KidsHealth: Food Allergies
kidshealth.org/en/parents/food-allergies.html
This website explains what allergies are and the problems they can cause.

BOOKS

Duhig, Holly. *Understanding Allergies.* New York, NY: PowerKids Press, 2019.

Gulati, Annette. *Life With Food Allergies.* Mankato, MN: Child's World, 2019.

LaPlante, Walter. *I'm Allergic to Tree Nuts.* New York, NY: Gareth Stevens Publishing, 2019.

Publisher's note to educators and parents: Our editors have carefully reviewed these websites to ensure that they are suitable for students. Many websites change frequently, however, and we cannot guarantee that a site's future contents will continue to meet our high standards of quality and educational value. Be advised that students should be closely supervised whenever they access the Internet.

INDEX